Quilling For Christmas Gifts

Let's Study About Quilling And Learn How To Quill To Decorate Your Christmas Gifts

Copyright © 2020

All rights reserved.

DEDICATION

The author and publisher have provided this e-book to you for your personal use only. You may not make this e-book publicly available in any way. Copyright infringement is against the law. If you believe the copy of this e-book you are reading infringes on the author's copyright, please notify the publisher at: https://us.macmillan.com/piracy

Contents

What Is Paper Quilling?.. 1

How To Make: Paper quilling Christmas 7

What Is Paper Quilling?

Paper quilling is a favorite crafting pastime but is by no means new. This paper art has existed since the invention of paper. Paper quilling is the art of cutting paper into long thin strips, rolling and pinching the pieces into different shapes, and then gluing the shapes together to form decorative art. Paper quilling projects can be used to decorate cards, boxes, gift bags, picture frames, or even be made into 3D stand-alone art pieces.

Your imagination only limits the possibilities. The decorative pieces can be simple or complex, but one thing is for sure, paper quilling can be mastered in an hour or two. Quilling is the perfect craft project for beginners. It is easy for a novice paper crafter to get good results, and another plus is the fact that this craft costs almost next to nothing to make.

The History of Paper Quilling

The origins of this artwork are not known. Some people believe that quilling was started in China after the invention of paper, and others think the craft had its origins in the 13th century. Nuns would imitate the iron decoration that was used as metal ornamentation in home decor. They would roll strips of gilded paper cut from books. The paper filigree designs were then used to decorate books and religious objects.

Paper quilling then resurged in popularity in the 18th century as a "suitable" pastime for the women of the aristocracy. The art of quilling spread from Europe to America and was favored by the American colonists as a decorative method. Quilling has had a resurgence in popularity, and it has been raised to an art form today.

Fun Fact

During the time of the Renaissance, Italian and French monks and nuns would use quilling to decorate book covers and other religious items.

Tools Required for Paper Quilling

Beginning quilling can be accomplished using only strips of paper, a toothpick, knitting needle or similar object, and some glue. If you get bitten by the quilling bug, you can invest in proper quilling tools to make your job that much easier.

Paper Quilling Strips: Precut paper designed especially for quilling can be bought online or at your local craft store. The advantage of using pre-cut paper is that your paper strips will always be the same width and of course you will also save time when using this type of paper.

Slotted Tool: This tool is a handle with a comfort grip that has a slotted metal piece at the top to insert your paper strips and then twists them into circular shapes. This tool makes it easier to control and roll your paper strips.

Tweezers: Tweezers are handy for holding your quilled shapes together while you are applying glue.

Needle Tool: The needle tool is a handle with a comfort grip that has a needle on one end. This tool is useful for applying glue to the ends of your paper strips.

Circle Sized Ruler: This handy tool is a ruler that has various sized holes in the middle. Place your rolled paper coil into a hole and get an accurate measurement.

Curling Coach: This tool is similar to the sized circle ruler. It makes the job of curling paper easy. It is especially useful when used in conjunction with the slotted tool.

Crimper Tool: This tool adds some crimped texture to your paper strips. Crimping adds interest to your quilling design.

White Glue: Most quillers use ordinary PVA glue.

Notable Paper Quilling Artists

Are you looking for some inspirations to help you kick-start your projects? Make sure to view some of the works of these artists.

Yulia Brodskaya: Yulia is a Russian born paper artist that fell in love with quilling in 2006 and hasn't stopped since. She started out as an illustrator and graphic artist but changed to paper art after her first paper project. She needed to design an original display for her name on a brochure and used quilling. The rest is history. Yulia's art is beautiful, quirky and utterly delightful!

Farah Al Fardh: Farah is an Emirati artist and trailblazer in the Arabic world when it comes to paper art. She became the first Emirati and Arab to be awarded the 'Certificate of Accreditation from The Quilling Guild in the UK and continued to wow the world with her creative pieces. She especially likes to make whimsical 3-d quilling sculptures. Be sure to visit her YouTube channel.

Ann Martin: Ann Martin is an author and paper art enthusiast that specializes in "custom quilled marriage certificates, ketubot, and wedding invitation mats that are suitable for framing, as well as paper jewelry." She has a website that focuses on quilling and other types of paper arts. I particularly like the site because Ann features high-quality paper arts and artists, and is an excellent source of information if you want to keep up with current trends in the world of paper crafting.

Connect With Other Quillers

If you want to learn more about the art of paper quilling, an excellent place to start is by joining a quilling guild. The premier guild is the Quilling Guild of the UK.

Although the guild hosts events that are in Great Britain, you can still become an online member and receive their publications (digital version) even if you live elsewhere in the world.

You can always find or start a club with like-minded people who enjoy the craft if you want to meet locally. It is a chance to share interests, improve your crafting skills and develop lifelong friendships.

Quilling For Christmas Gifts

How To Make: Paper quilling Christmas

Paper quilling is the art of rolling up strips of paper to produce decorative shapes. Here's how to use it to create lovely Christmas cards

What is quilling?

Quilling has been practised for centuries, but it's only in recent years that a choice of narrow paper strips have been readily available for use in this craft technique. Quilling paper strips are available in 3mm, 5mm and 1cm widths, or you can cut your own from a sheet of paper, either using a ruler and craft knife, a guillotine or a paper shredder.

Use the different widths and lengths of paper, then once they are rolled into coils they can be shaped into squares, diamonds, triangles, hearts, teardrops hearts and swirls.

You can buy specialist quilling tools, which have a protruding dowel with a slot to slip your paper strip into to start coiling. The tools are available with different depths to match the width of paper. The protruding dowels also differ in width so you can vary the size of the hole in the centre of the coil.

But don't worry if you don't have the specialist tools for quilling, you can improvise by wrapping the paper round a cocktail stick, which is what we've done for our project

Practice rolling strips of paper into coils using a cocktail stick. Twirl the stick with one hand, keeping the strip in place with the other, keeping it tight until you come to the end of the strip.

Slip the coil off then use another cocktail stick to apply a little glue to the open end. To make a relaxed coil, wind first onto the cocktail stick, then leave it to loosen, wind a bit more, leave to loosen and so on.

Experiment with the relaxed coils to make different shapes.

How to make the paper quilling shapes

Diamond

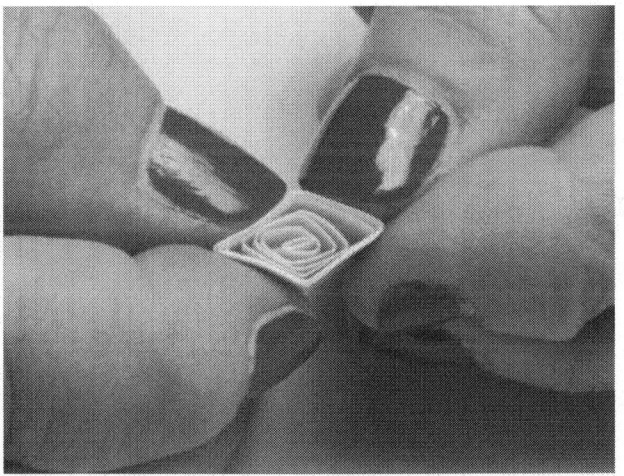

Press the coil flat between your thumb and forefinger, release the coil. Then reposition your thumb and forefinger over the pointed ends, and press flat again. Open the diamond shape out.

Teardrop

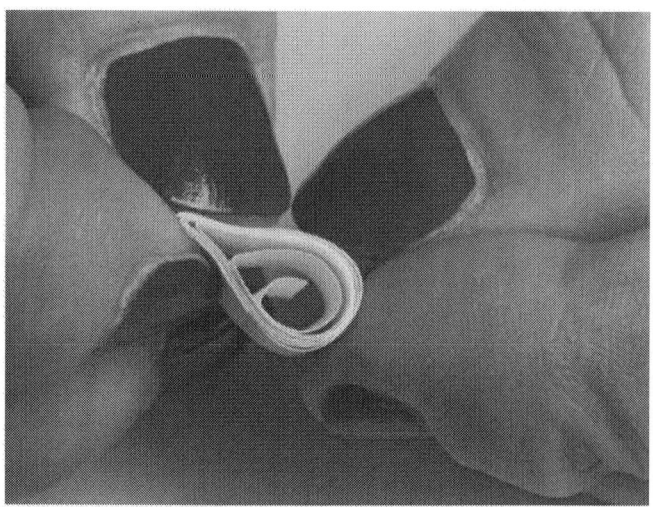

Pinch the coil at one end, using your thumb and forefinger, to create a point.

Quilling For Christmas Gifts

Eye

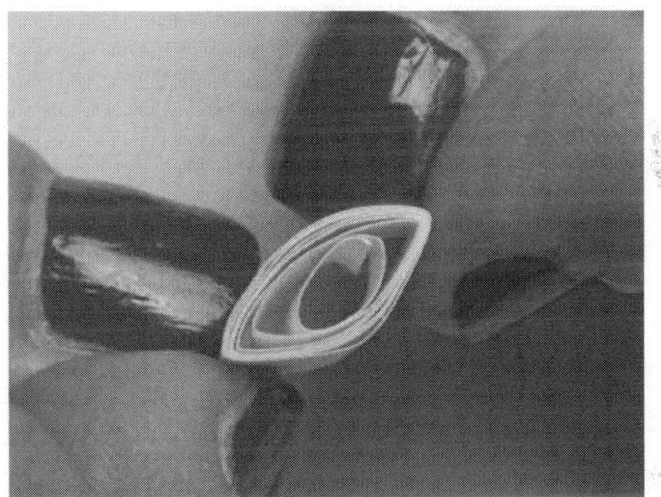

Pinch the coil at both ends using your thumbs and forefingers.

Square

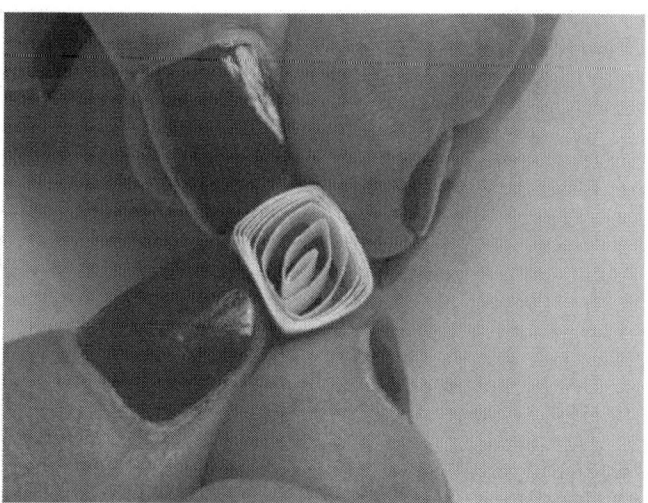

Make an eye shape, then pinch the other two sides to form a square.

Tight heart

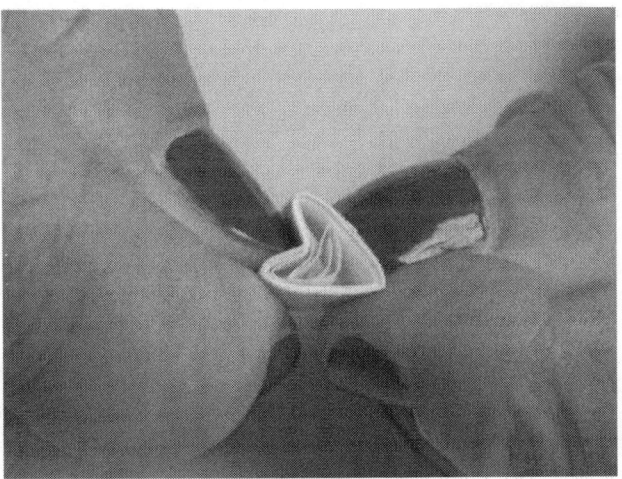

Make a teardrop then put a dent in the rounded end using your thumbnail.

Loose heart

Fold a strip in half, twist one end round a cocktail stick then roll loosely by hand until you have created one half of a heart. Repeat this step on the other end, rolling the strip in the opposite direction.

For all three paper quilling cards, you will need

- Strips of paper
- Cocktail stick
- PVA glue

How to make a mint green snowflake paper quilling card

We used 5mm-wide strips and a 15 x 10.5cm grey card blank

Quilling For Christmas Gifts

You will need

Large snowflake:

- 12 x 30cm mint green strips

Medium snowflake:

- 6 x 30cm mint green strips
- 6 x 20cm grey strips

Tiny snowflake

- 6 x 15cm mint green strips

Instructions

1. Roll six tight coils from mint paper, glue and set to one side. Roll six loose coils, glue then pinch them to make diamonds.

2. Apply a little glue to the edges of the six diamonds and stick them together to form the snowflake. Glue six tight coils in between each diamond.

3. Repeat to make the medium snowflake, using grey paper to make the tight coils.

4. Finally make the tiny snowflake and glue all three snowflakes to the front of the card.

Top tip: Using a pair of tweezers can help when picking up your coils and gluing them in place.

We used 1cm-wide strips, a 10.5cm square lilac card blank and a 8cm square piece of mint green paper.

You will need

- 14 x 30cm white strips

Instructions

1. Roll five tight coils, glue and set to one side. Roll five loose coils, glue then pinch them to make eye shapes.

2. Glue all five eye shapes together to form the snowflake. Then glue the five tight coils in between each eye shape.

3. Roll a further four loose coils and pinch to make them into teardrops.

4. Glue the snowflake to the centre of the mint green paper and

a teardrop in each corner. Then glue to the front of the lilac card front.

How to make a blue, white and grey snowflake paper quilling card

We used a combination of 1cm-wide and 5mm-wide strips, a 15cm square pale blue card blank and a 10cm square piece of metallic blue paper.

You will need

- 6 x 30cm white strips (1cm-wide)
- 6 x 20cm blue strips (5mm)
- 1 x 10cm blue strip (5mm)

- 6 x 20cm grey strips (5mm)

Instructions

1. Roll three tight grey coils, and three tight blue coils, glue and set to one side. Roll six loose white coils, glue then pinch into teardrops.

2. Roll the shorter strip of blue paper into a tight coil, glue, then stick the white teardrops around the edge. Then glue alternating grey and blue coils in between the six teardrops.

3. Make three loose grey hearts and three loose blue hearts. Glue the coils of the hearts to the snowflake, so the points of the hearts face out.

4. Stick the snowflake centrally on the blue metallic paper, then stick to the card front.

How to Make A Quilled Christmas Wreath Card

The Christmas season is here, and along with it comes the yearly rush to send out and give away holiday cards to your friends and family members. When it comes to Christmas cards, some of us like to go with the old stand-by box sets (JAM offers several lovely options) while others like to take the homemade route. If you are more prone to put yourself into the later category, this post is for you.

Those who keep up to date with paper crafting trends are probably familiar with quilling. For those who are not, here is a short explanation. Quilling is the practice of curling ans shaping strips of paper in order to create larger decorative shapes and designs. Here, I will show you how to use quilling to make your own beautiful and decorative Christmas wreath cards!

You will need:

- One standard quilling tool (A sewing needle will also work.)
- Bright Hue Green Paper
- Bright Hue Red Paper
- Dark Red Paper
- White Paper or Cardstock

- Scissors
- One hot glue gun (with glue)

Step 1:

Cut thin, 11 inch long strips of green paper. These strips should be roughly even in width, but they do not need to be exact.

Step 2:

Using your quilling tool or needle, roll the first strip of paper into a spiral. After it is fully rolled, remove it from the tool and let it partially unravel. It should look like this.

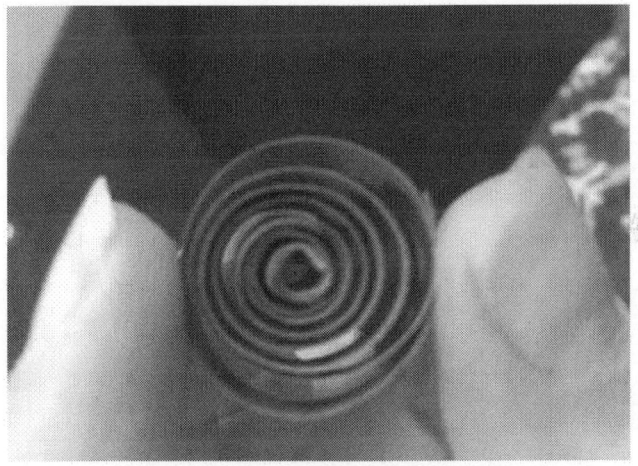

Glue the loose end of the spiral in place with your glue gun. Repeat this step until you have enough green spirals to form a full wreath.

Step 3:

Choose a sheet or paper or card stock to use as the body of your card. For durability, card stock is recommended. Before gluing them in place, lay put your green spirals on your card surface as you would like to appear in your finished product.

After your design has been decided, use your glue gun to glue your wreath together on the card's surface!

Step 4:

Now that your basic wreath shape is completed, you can move on to making the bow. To begin the bow, cut several strips of red and dark red paper and you did with the green paper in step 1. After these strips have been cut, choose two strips of the same color to make into quilled teardrop shapes. These will become the inner most pieces of the bow.

Step 5:

To create a tear, or raindrop shape, wind your strip of paper around your quilling tool or needle in the same way that you did to create basic circles. When removing the paper from the tool, only allow it to unravel part way instead of letting it go. The degree to which you allow it to unravel will affect the size of your tear shape.

After this spiral has partially loosened, hold the center of this spiral with the index finger and thumb of your non-dominant hand while pulling gently outward and using your dominant hand to pull the outer portion of the spiral in the opposite direction while pinching to form a point (the top of the teardrop). Glue the loose end of the shape in place with your glue gun.

Step 6:

After you have made two tear drop shapes of the same color, take two strips of another shape of red and tightly wrap them around these shapes. Glue the loose ends in place. Next, take two strips of the first shade of red you used and loosely wrap them around the outer surface of the shapes you just wrapped. Pinch the top of each one so that it matches the shapes of the center pieces. To finish the two halves of the top of the bow, do this again with the opposite shade of red. Shown below is the tear-drop shape you started with compared to a fully completed half of a bow.

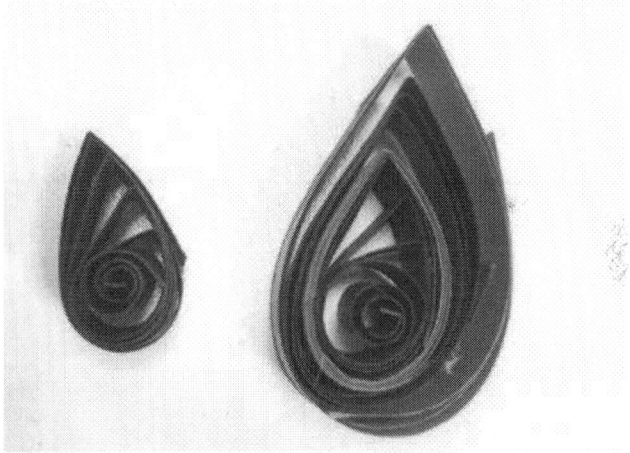

Step 7:

Make a middle for your bow by winding a tight, small circle of red paper and wrapping a strip of the other other red shade around it. Glue this round shape together with your glue gun and then glue all ribbon pieces onto the wreath in any way you would like!

After these are in place, loosely curl a few more red strips of paper and glue them in place to create the bottom/ excess bow strings.

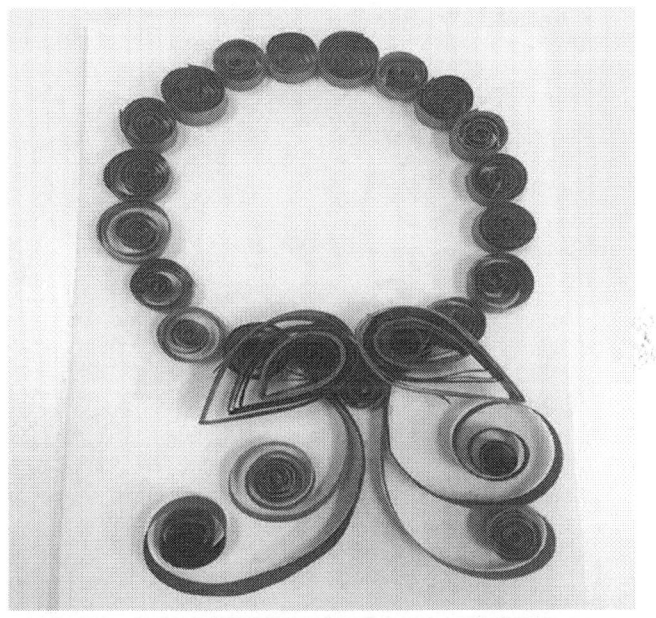

Your wreath card is now complete! If you wish, you may use writing utensils to include a message such as "Merry Christmas", "Happy Holidays", or "Hi, Mom" within the wreath!

We hope that this craft helped to brighten up your season. Happy Holidays from all of us at JAM!

How to Make a Christmas Paper Quilling Snowman Craft

Summary: Christmas crafts are popular and good gifts. Today, I will tell you how to make a Christmas paper quilling snowman.

There are many quilling paper Christmas ornaments on Pandahall. Nearly all of them are cute and easy to make. Today's project is a paper quilling snowman. The main materials are quilling papers in different colors and some blue pearl beads. You need no other professional skills in making this DIY snowman craft. Now, follow me to make this Christmas snowman.

Supplies in making this Christmas paper quilling snowman craft:

3MM Blue Pearl Beads
Quilling Paper (Bright Red, Green, Yellow, Black, White)
Model
Scissor
Tweezer

White Glue
Rolling Pen

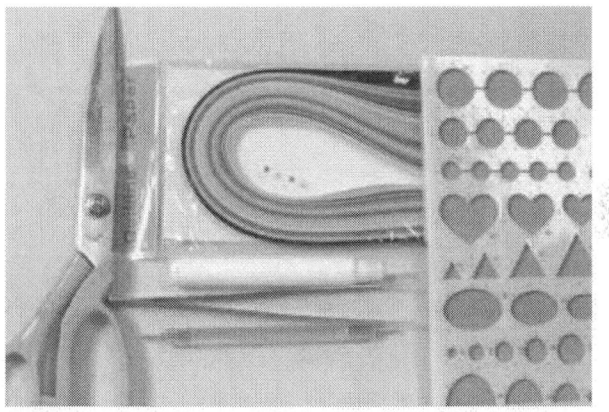

Step 1: Make several paper quilling circular beads

1st, take about 4 pieces of white quilling papers, roll them into a big circular beads and stick the end firmly;

2nd, take about 2 pieces of white quilling papers, roll them into a circular bead, then make the other 5 white circular beads and other 2 red circular beads, and 2 green circular beads with the same length;

3rd, stick all the small circular beads around the big circular bead as pictured.

Step 2: Add another circular pattern and pearl beads

1st, roll a white circular bead with about 3 pieces of quilling papers, stick 2 3mm blue pearl beads on it as eyes;

> 2nd, cut a short piece of yellow quilling paper, roll it to a circular bead, make assure the inner part higher than the outer part, then stick it to the white circular bead as a mouth as pictured.

Step 3: Make an oval bead

Roll a black quilling paper into a circular bead, put it into the 10cm hole and stick the end, and pinch the circular bead into an oval bead as pictured.

Step 4: Make the final Christmas snowman design

1st, stick the black oval bead to the head of the snowman as hat, then roll other black circular bead and stick it to the hat as pictured;

Quilling For Christmas Gifts

2nd, cut a short red quilling paper and a black quilling paper, roll them several circle and loosen them to make them as the picture shown;

3rd, stich the end of the red quilling paper with the black quilling paper together, then stick the end to left circular beads of the snowman, and stick 3 blue pearl beads on the big circular bead as pictured.

Here is the final look of the Christmas paper quilling snowman:

Do you love this colorful and cute paper quilling snowman? I finished this DIY snowman craft within just 15minutes. You can also learn to make a Christmas snowman at home. It is appropriate for a new comer to start his/her quilling paper DIY journey. Now, my tutorial on how to make a Christmas snowman has come to an end. Have a nice try!

How to Make a Purple Quilling Paper Flower Necklace With White Pearl Beads Decorated

Introduction: How to Make a Purple Quilling Paper Flower Necklace With White Pearl Beads Decorated

About: Hi, guys!! I'm Daisy. I love putting beads together to make jewelry work; sharing jewelry designs. If you like jewelry and beads, you are in the right place.

This article is about a purple quilling paper flower necklace. It's not very difficult to make the purple quilling paper flower necklace. Just check the tutorial below.

Step 1: Supplies Needed in DIY the Purple Quilling Paper Flower Necklace:

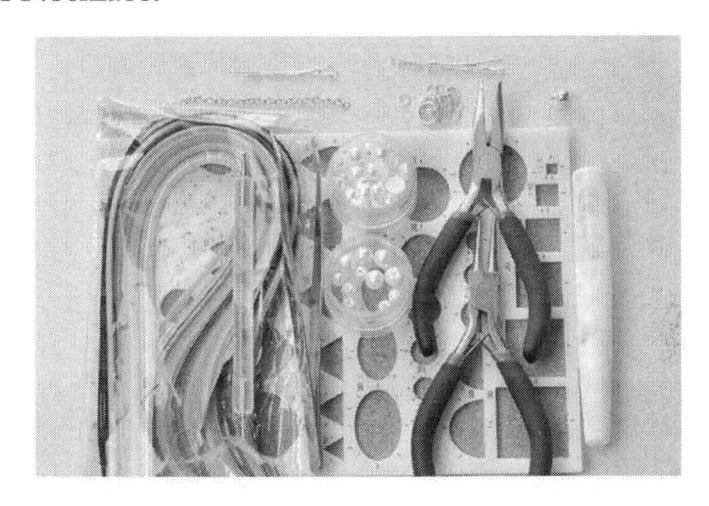

DIY Paper Quilling Strips Sets

10mm White Round Pearl Beads

8mm White Round Pearl Beads

6mm White Round Pearl Beads

White Flat Round Pearl Cabochons

Iron Cross Chains

Silver Jump Rings

Silver Headpins

Silver Eyepins

11.5x6mm Silver Round Magnetic Clasps

Needle Nose Plier

Round Nose Plier

Rolling Pen

Tweezers

White Glue

Step 2: Make the First Part of the Purple Quilling Paper Flower Necklace

Quilling For Christmas Gifts

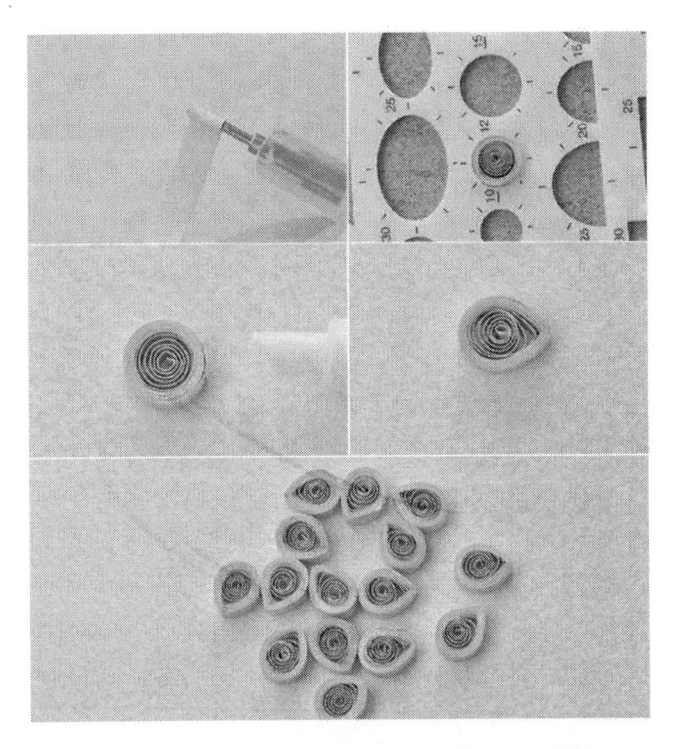

1st, cut a piece of purple quilling paper and use rolling pen to make a circular pattern (as shown in the picture);

2nd, use white glue to fix the circular pattern and glue the ends (as shown in the picture);

3rd, make the circular pattern into a drop pattern (as shown in the picture);

4th, refer to the above steps to make more such drop patterns (as shown in the picture);

Step 3:

5th, use white glue to combine 5 purple drop patterns into a flower (as shown in the picture);

6th, refer to the above steps to make two more purple quilling paper flowers (as shown in the picture);

7th, use white glue to glue a white flat round pearl cabochon onto the middle part of the three purple quilling paper flowers respectively (as shown in the picture).

Step 4: Make the Rest Part of the Purple Quilling Paper Flower Necklace

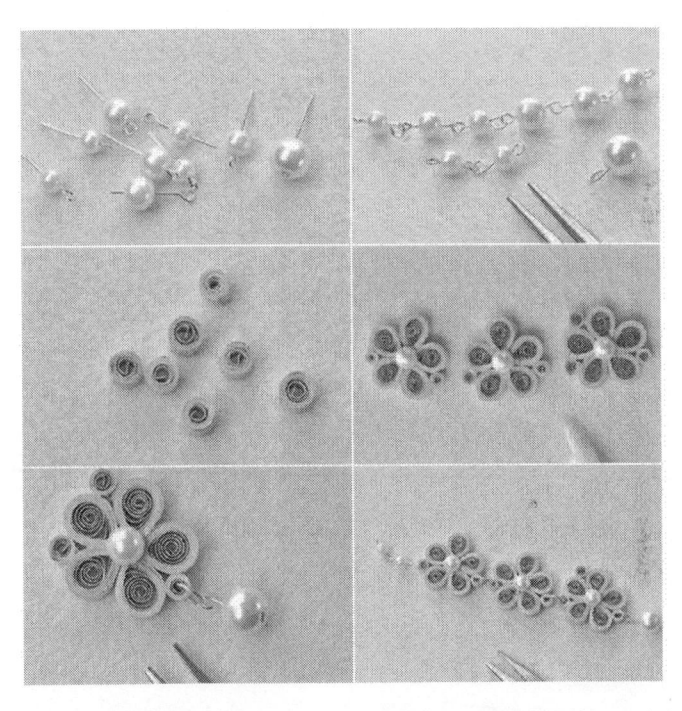

1st, combine a 10mm white round pearl bead, 3 8mm white round pearl beads and 5 6mm white round pearl beads with silver eyespins one by one(as shown in the picture);

2nd, make a hoop on the other end of the silver eyepins. Then, combine 3 6mm white round pearl beads with 3 8mm white round pearl beads. Then, combine two 6mm white round pearl beads together(as shown in the picture);

3rd, refer to Step1 to make 7 more purple circular quilling paper patterns (as shown in the picture);

4th, add a purple circular quilling paper patterns on the two sides of a purple quilling paper flower. Repeat this step once. Then, add the other three purple circular quilling paper patterns to the other purple quilling paper flower(as shown in the picture);

5th, add the 10mm white round pearl bead to the hole of the purple circular quilling paper pattern through a silver jump ring(as shown in the picture);

6th, add the other two purple quilling paper flowers and two 6mm white round pearl beads pattern through silver jump rings (as shown in the picture);

Step 5:

7th, add the 6 white round pearl beads pattern to the hole of the other purple circular pattern through a silver jump ring(as shown in the picture);

8th, cut two parts of silver twisted chain (about the same length) and add them to the two sides respectively (as shown in the picture);

9th, combine the two ends of the purple quilling paper flower necklace together through an 11.5x6mm silver round magnetic clasp and two silver jump rings(as shown in the picture).

Step 6: Here Is the Final Look of the Purple Quilling Paper Flower Necklace.

What do you think of this purple quilling paper flower necklace with white pearl beads decorated? The purple quilling paper flower necklace looks very elegant. The three quilling paper flowers are not difficult to make. Just collect some materials and give it a try!

Simple Tutorial on Chain Necklace with Quilling Flowers

Hello, friends. Have you any interest for quilling jewelry? How about quilling flower necklace? If you are searching for quilling jewelry, then I think you will be excited after seeing this tutorial. Today, I am going to show you a project on how to make a chain necklace with flowers. Then let's see the making details.

Supplies needed in making chain necklace with quilling flower:
3mm quilling paper
5mm quilling paper
6x3mm white acrylic pearl cabochons
8mm white glass pearl beads
brass jump rings
brass ball headpins
bronze lobster claw clasp
iron cross chain

scissors
glue gun
tweezers
white glue
needle nose pliers
round nose pliers

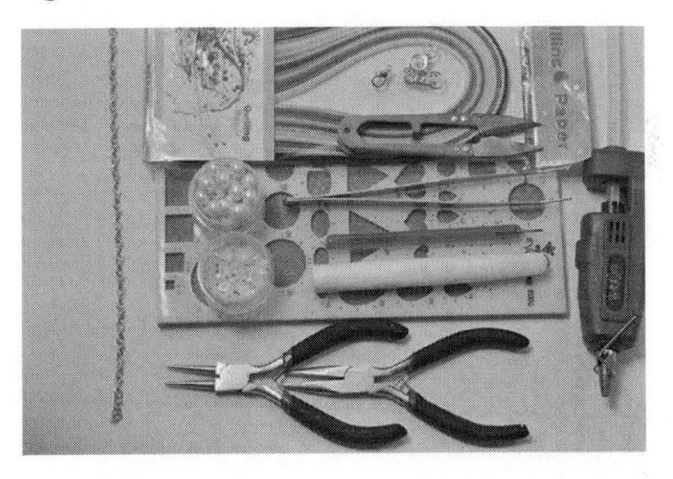

Step 1: make quilling flowers

Firstly, roll a piece of orange paper around the needle nose plier and make them in round shape.

Secondly, continue to make many roll patterns like it, then combine five pieces with glue.

Thirdly, add a white acrylic pearl cabochon onto the center of the flower pattern and stick them tightly with glue. Then make another same three flower patterns.

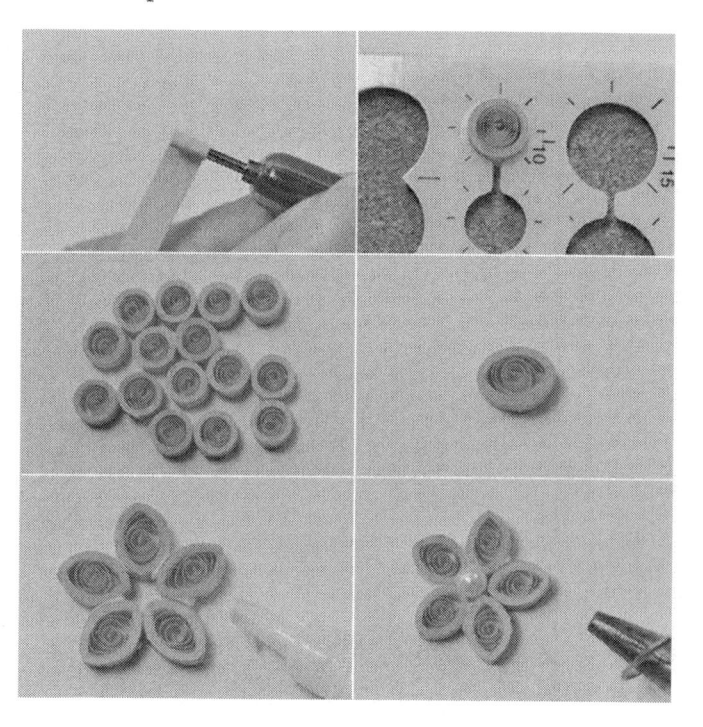

Step 2: add chain and pearl dangles

Firstly, cut off the chain with suitable length according to your neck. Secondly, add a jump ring to the roll quilling pattern separately.

Then add them onto the chain on the suitable position.

Thirdly, slide 5 pearl beads onto the headpins respectively and make a loop at the end. Then add the pearl dangles to the chain like this picture did.

Step 3: finish this chain necklace

Firstly, add a jump ring and a lobster claw clasp on the ends of chain. Then connect the both ends.

Secondly, add a pearl bead dangle on the excess chain, please see this pictures.

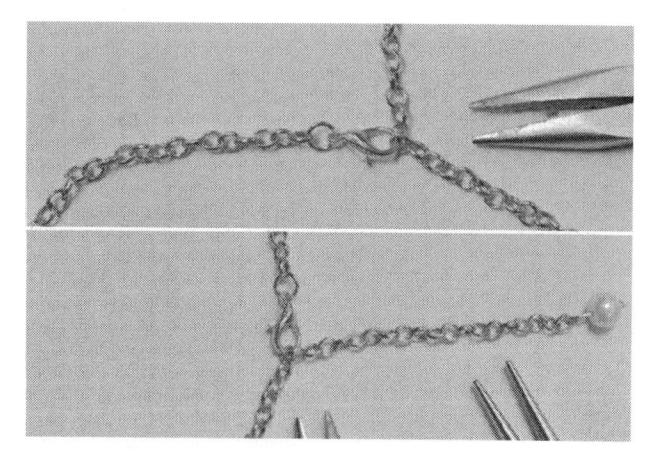

Then this chain necklace with quilling flowers has been finished!

Quilling For Christmas Gifts

Such a beautiful necklace, do you think so? Try to make one for yourself if you like it, pretty things always deserve your time and energy. Hope you have a wonderful time!

DIY Paper Quilling Christmas Tree Ornament

List of Supplies:

- Green Craft paper

- Quilling strips in different colors
- Quilling Tool
- Pencil or pen
- Scissors
- Craft glue or glue stick

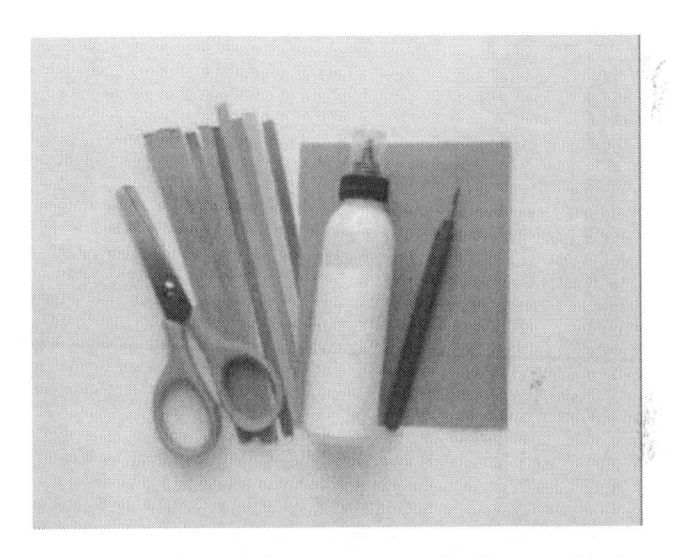

Instructions for making the Paper Quilling Christmas Tree Ornament:

1. Take a 6 inches long green quilling strip and use the slotted quilling tool to coil the entire strip into a tight coil.

2. Remove the coiled strip from the tool and allow it loosen up a little. Prepare a total of 15 similar loose coils.

Quilling For Christmas Gifts

3. Use 3.5 inch red quilling strips to make small teardrop shapes.

Quilling For Christmas Gifts

4. Now make a few coils using quilling strips in assorted colors. You can make them loose or tight – whatever you like. Make four brown loose coils as well.

5. Take a rectangular piece of green craft paper and gather all the green loose coils prepared in step 1 and 2. Use craft glue to stick 5 loose coils in a straight line, towards the lower side of the green colored craft paper.

6. Continue sticking rows of the loose green coils, one above the other. As you move upward, keep reducing the number of coils in a line by 1, so that you end up with a triangle pattern.

Quilling For Christmas Gifts

7. Stick the red teardrop shapes on the top end of the triangle. Glue them together with the pointy end out, so you get a 5 point star pattern.

Quilling For Christmas Gifts

8. Okay, your tree is nearly ready! Cut the craft paper along the outer edge of the Christmas tree, including the red star.

9. Use the assorted colorful coils to decorate the tree, by simply gluing them on either side. Add 4 brown coils on the bottom side of the tree in a square pattern to make the tree trunk.

10. Finally add a small bead on the center of the star pattern if you like. Let it dry and it's done!

Quilling For Christmas Gifts

This DIY Paper Quilling Christmas Tree Ornament is quite multipurpose. Of course, you can attach a string and hang it on the tree with an equally cute Paper Quilled Wreath Ornament, but you can also make a handmade Christmas Card with it. Or, why not attach it to a piece of card to make it go with these Christmas Gift Tags? See, a little effort and a few strips sure go a long way!

Quilled Christmas Lights Craft – Kids Christmas Craft Activity

Are you looking for a unique craft to do with your kids? This would even be a great craft to do with kids for a Winter or Christmas party. With just a few tools they can make this unique set of lights to display for the holidays!

A few years ago I helped with my son's 5th grade Christmas party and this would have been a great craft for them to work on.

Quilling For Christmas Gifts

(Please note the links below are Amazon affiliate links. I will earn a small commission if you make a purchase using my link.)

List of Supplies:

1. Craft paper – white
2. Quilling Strips
3. Slotted Paper Quilling Tools
4. Scissors
5. Craft Glue or glue stick

Quilling For Christmas Gifts

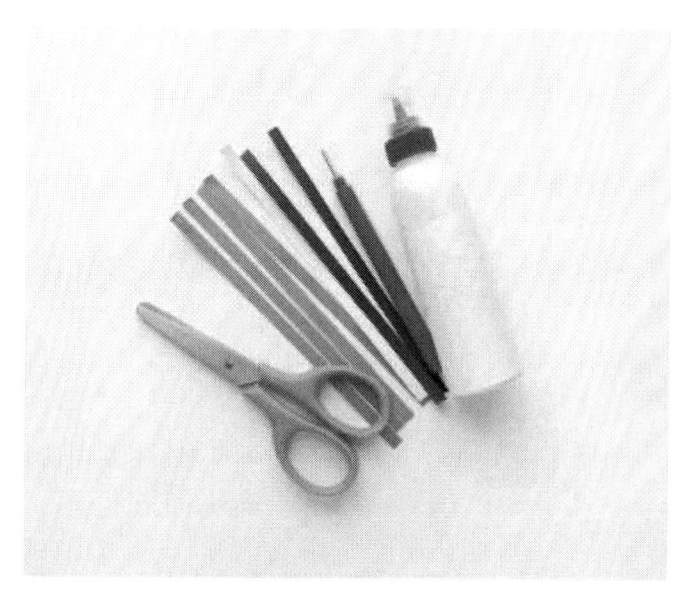

Instructions to make the craft:

Quilling For Christmas Gifts

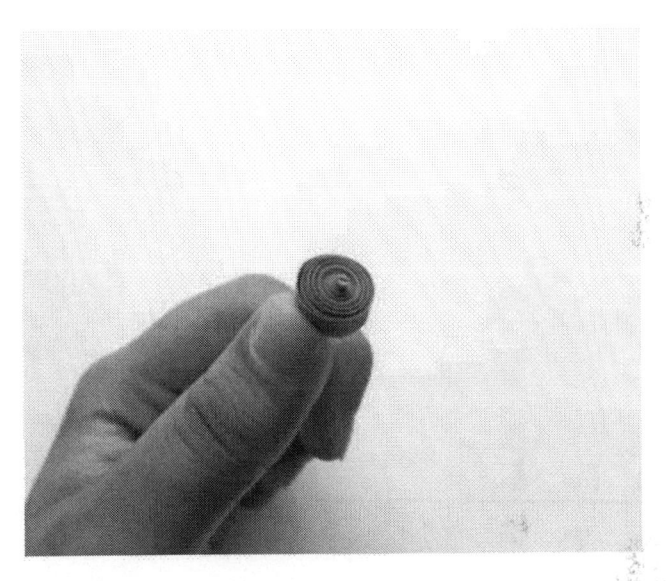

Step 1: Take a 20 inches long colored quilling strip and use the slotted quilling tool to coil the entire strip.

Step 2: Once the coiling is done, take out the coiled strip from the tool and allow it loosen up.

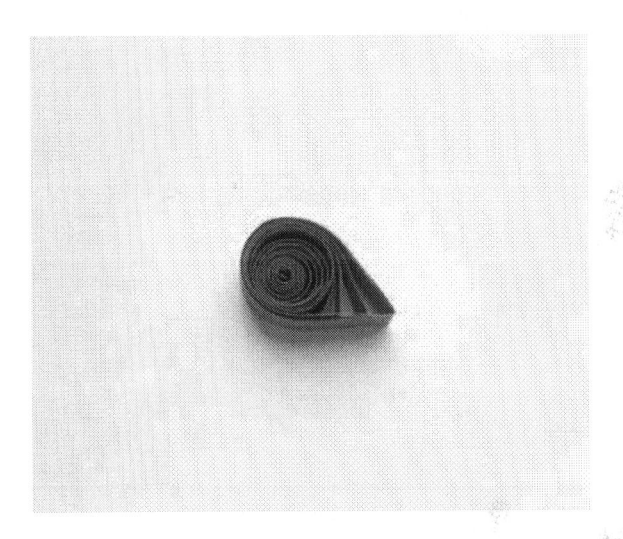

Step 3: Press any one side of the loose coil to form a teardrop shape and glue the open end to secure the shape.

Quilling For Christmas Gifts

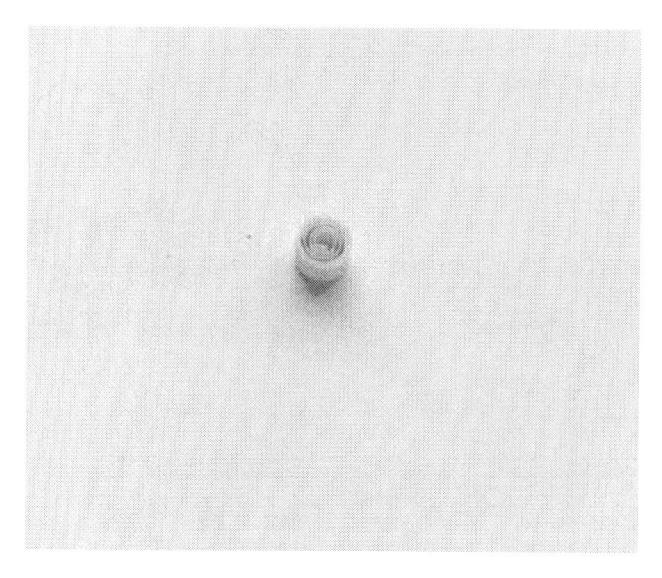

Step 4: Take a 3 inches long white colored quiling strip and create a loose coil shape with it.

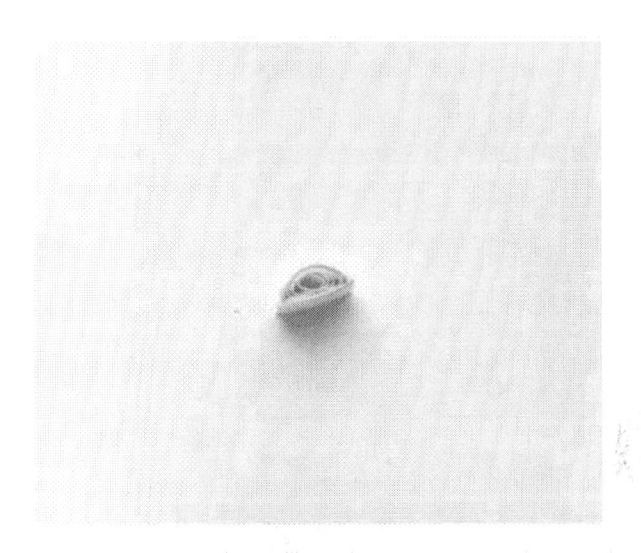

Step 5: Press 2 opposite sides of the loose coil to form a lens shape.

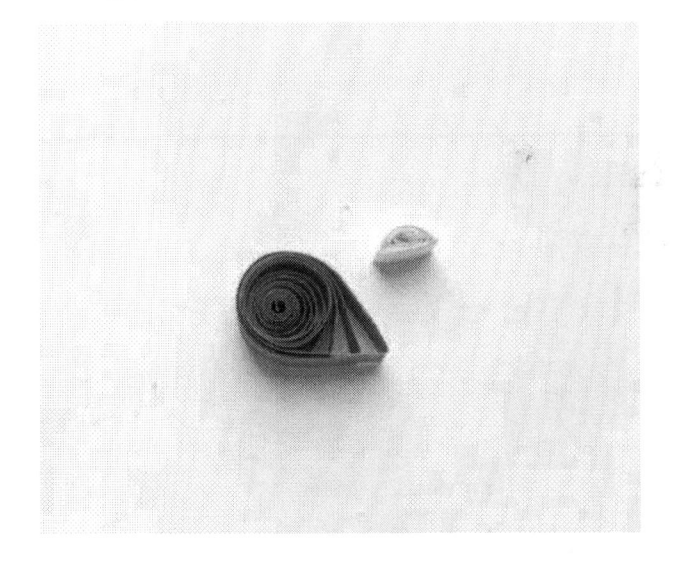

Step 6:Grab the teardrop shape prepared in the previous steps.

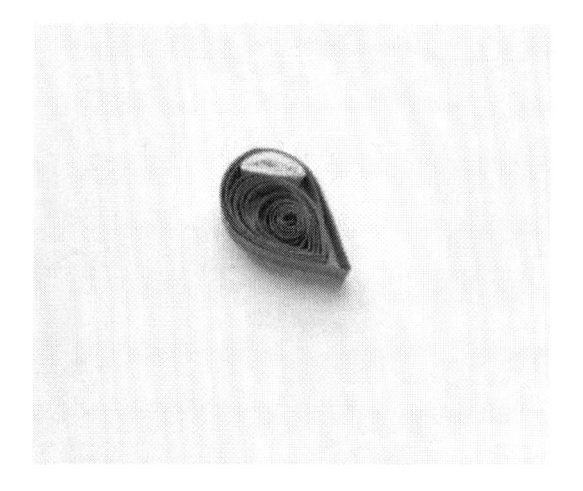

Step 7: Insert the lens shape created in step 5 into the teardrop shape, through the gap of any coils near the curved end; the bulb pattern is ready. Similarly create more bulb patterns.

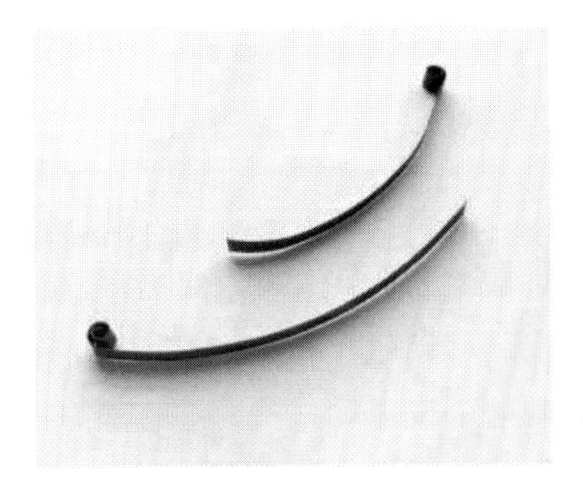

Step 8: Now take a 6 inches long black quilling strip and create a small twirl on any of its ends. Use about 2 or 3 cm to create the twirl pattern.

Step 9: Cut out a white craft paper or cardstock paper for the background, or you can choose any color you want.

Step 10: Glue the 2 black twirled strips on the paper by creating a slight curvy pattern with them. Glue the 2 strips in 2 rows, keeping at least an inch gap between them.

Quilling For Christmas Gifts

Step 11: Take a bulb pattern and glue it on the paper by keeping the curved end adjacent to the black strip (which is the main wire for the bulbs).

Step 12: One by one add the rest of the bulbs to fill the black strip.

Allow the glue to dry and have fun!

Made in the USA
Monee, IL
19 October 2023